TOPS
WITH A
TWIST

TOPS
WITH A
TWIST

INTERWEAVE PRESS

Project editor, Judith Durant
Spin·Off editor, Deborah Robson
Technical editor, Dorothy T. Ratigan

Photography, Joe Coca
Cover design, Sage Graphics
Illustrations, Susan Strawn, Gayle Ford

Interweave Press
201 East Fourth Street
Loveland, Colorado 80537
USA

Printed in the United States of America by Vision Graphics

First printing: 5M:999:VG

Contents

Introduction 7

Abbreviations and Techniques 11

Shaded Lattice Hat 16

Big Mac Crochet Beret 20

Circles with a Spark 24

"Maybelline" Hat 27

Acorn Hat 30

Rainbow Lambs' Tails Cap 33

Turkish Braid Hat 36

Beaded Wonder 39

Bon-Bon Bowler 43

Jewels 46

Pearls Squared 49

Turkish Infant Cap 53

Twisted Tail Top 55

Fair Isle Tam 58

Highway Woman's Hat 62

Fool's Hat 66

Dreaming of the Garden 71

The Trickster's Hat 74

Index 79

Introduction

Hats may be the most personal item of clothing that humans have invented. Rules of etiquette apply in different ages and locations: men may be required to doff them before entering certain buildings, women may be compelled to don them before entering others. Often we take them for granted. We grab them from a rack in the hall to keep the rain or snow off, throw them in the corner when we don't need them, and use them to declare status or formality or kinship with a group of similar hat-wearers. Hats can be serious business, but they're also playful.

When Interweave Press asked the staff of *Spin·Off* magazine to come up with an idea for a contest that would tap its readers' creativity, the focus formed quickly. Through the conference we sponsor every fall, the *Spin·Off* Autumn Retreat (SOAR), we were familiar with some of the vision and talent available within this community, and we'd seen a lot of tantalizing headgear over the years.

We sent out a challenge to *Spin·Off* readers asking for hats. The hats had to be made of handspun yarn (this is a magazine for handspinners, after all), and the designs had to be original. We called the contest "Tops with a Twist."

About eight months passed between announcement and deadline. We waited and wondered. Spinning is labor-intensive, and creativity requires perking time. Because we have run contests for handspinners before and because we publish a magazine that features this group's efforts on a quarterly basis, we knew we would receive a broad variety and large number of entries, and that the level of inventiveness would be high, but beyond that . . . a mystery.

One hat arrived five months early, and we loved it. Most hats arrived in the flurry of packages just before the deadline. When judging day arrived, 132 "tops with a twist" were unwrapped and spread out on the long, blond oak tables in the third-floor conference room.

We had some idea of how we would judge the contest before the entries covered those tables, but changed the format almost immediately. The *Spin·Off* staff was so excited that we found excuses to go up and down the halls of the three-story building, suggesting that people from other departments "just come look." Everyone who entered the room ended up trying on hats. Each person was drawn to different types of hat. One person's "never on earth would I wear that" became another's "I love this!"—and usually the first person would then say, "Hey, that looks great on you!"

Clearly, we needed a large and diverse group

of judges, not the handful we had envisioned. We didn't want to represent one aesthetic or body type or style. We wanted to acknowledge the whole wild, wonderful world of hats.

Judging took place over two days and involved people from almost all of Interweave's departments. We moved a mirror into the room, and we gave each other feedback. "I think this is yours" and "I want to steal this one" became refrains. People came and went depending on workloads, but there were usually three or four people in the room, trying on hats, making comments, playing. Yes, serious spinners participated and they judged craftsmanship. But most of the judges for this contest did not spin themselves. To move forward in the contest, hats had to work both as creative efforts and as objects that human beings would actually wear, whether seriously or for fun.

We had only twelve prizes, and we had a lot more than twelve terrific hats. As the judging proceeded, the editors involved began to think of how they might recognize and share more of these great projects. We came up with more ways to win.

There would be the twelve "top hats," acknowledged with the prizes donated by a generous group of spinning suppliers. The creators of these hats would receive gift certificates and boxes of fiber and would be shown in the magazine.

Then we'd select hats to be featured in a special publication—the one you're holding. For this group, we looked for hats that would be knitted (with one crocheted exception) and that would be classic enough to appeal to the spinning and knitting communities. We would offer hats for men, women, and children, at gauges ranging from fine to bulky. A few of the twelve winners qualified under these criteria, but we also selected from the larger group.

Next, we pulled aside hats that would be used as projects in *Spin·Off* magazine. These could be less classic, since one of *Spin·Off*'s goals is to push textile limits and encourage "I've never seen that before" creative efforts. Finally, we gave up on the selection process entirely and decided to put together a slide show featuring all the hats, which would be available to spinning and knitting groups for use as a program. In the end, we had to declare that all the hats were winners.

What is it about spinning that produces such an outpouring of creativity? Backing up a step, why does anyone still make yarn by hand as we cross the threshold to the twenty-first century? Those of us who do this have all been told that you can actually buy yarn in a wide variety of colors, weights, textures, and fibers. It's ready to use for knitting, crochet, weaving, tatting, or whatever. Why make your own string?

Spinners have a few standard answers for these questions. They talk about the meditative aspect of the work itself, the control they have over the process (ability to choose color, weight, fiber blend, and so forth), and the community of handspinners, which is widespread and close-knit and cannot be overestimated as a source of support and encouragement.

At the bottom of this is that spinners are spoiled. Once you've worked with yarn you made yourself, you can only occasionally be tempted to go back to the machine-spun stuff. When you do succumb, you know so much more about what you're choosing that you tend to select only the finest commercial yarns. That's the range of materials you can make for yourself, even as a relatively inexperienced spinner.

A new spinner can quickly learn to spin unique, designer-quality yarns. (A few lessons from a knowledgeable spinner help a lot, although many spinners are self-taught.) As the spinner's control grows, so does a quality or skill that spinners demonstrate with reliable flair: creativity. A handspinner's yarn is often slightly different in gauge, materials, color, or quantity ("Oops, I'm going to run out" or "Yikes, I've got an extra pound") from what's called for in commercial patterns. If you can match the gauge on a pattern with your yarn (whether handspun or commercial), you can swap yarns. But spinners end up in situations that require creativity to resolve. And they find themselves in the company of other spinners who egg them on to try a crazy idea, to think through an apparently unsolvable problem, to make a project work despite setbacks.

Within the spinning individual and the spinning community, we have rampant creativity, a bunch of intrepid adventurers, and the skills to back up the vision. We do this stuff because it's fun. And we take textiles in interesting and unusual directions because we're so closely involved with every element of the process, from the individual fiber between one person's hands to the unique hat that ends up finding its perfect home on a specific head.

Then we share.

Welcome to the party. Whether you spin your own yarn to make one of these hats as written or use these ideas as sparks for your own creativity, you'll make hats as unique as these are, as individual as you are. Warm your head. Warm your loved ones' noggins.

Hats off to play, and grace, and honor, and to all the worlds of meaning and frivolity in this most odd and fanciful and traditional and idiosyncratic of garments. Enjoy your discovery of eighteen of the best.

Deborah Robson
Editor, *Spin·Off* magazine
August, 1999

Abbreviations and Techniques

Abbreviations

Here are some abbreviations and techniques you'll find used in some of the patterns presented here. Stitches unique to a given hat are explained within the pattern.

beg	beginning; begin; begins
BO	bind off
bet	between
CC	contrasting color
ch	chain
cm	centimeter(s)
CO	cast on
dc	double crochet
dec(s)	decrease(s); decreasing
dpn	double-pointed needles
inc	increase(s); increasing
k	knit
k2tog	knit two stitches together
kwise	knitwise
MC	main color
mm	millimeter(s)
M1	make one (increase)
p	purl
psso	pass slipped stitch over
rem	remain; remains; remaining
rep	repeat
rev St st	reverse stockinette stitch
rib	ribbing
RS	right side
sc	single crochet
sk	skip
sl	slip
sl st	slip stitch
ssk	slip 1 kwise, slip 1 kwise, k2 sl sts tog tbl
st(s)	stitch(es)
St st	stockinette stitch
tbl	through back loop
tog	together
WS	wrong side
wyb	with yarn in back
wyf	with yarn in front
yo	yarn over
*	repeat starting point (i.e., rep from *)

Reading charts

Unless otherwise indicated, charts are read from the bottom up. When knitting in the round, read chart from right to left for all rows.

Crochet stitches

Chain stitch (ch): Make a slipknot on the hook. Yarn over the hook and draw it through the loop of the slipknot. Repeat, drawing the yarn through the last loop formed.

Crochet chain stitch

Double crochet (dc): Yarn over hook, insert the hook into a stitch, yarn over the hook (figure 1)

Double crochet figure 1

and draw a loop through the stitch (three loops on hook), yarn over the hook and draw it through two loops, yarn over the hook and draw it through the remaining two loops (figure 2).

*Double crochet
figure 2*

Single crochet (sc): Insert the hook into a stitch, yarn over the hook and draw a loop through the stitch, yarn over the hook (figure 1) and draw it through both loops on the hook (figure 2).

*Single crochet
figure 1*

*Single crochet
figure 2*

Slip stitch (sl st): Insert the hook into a stitch, yarn over the hook and draw a loop through the stitch on the hook.

Slip stitch crochet

To join a round with a slip stitch, insert the hook into the first stitch, yarn over and draw a loop through the work and the stitch on the hook.

Slip stitch join

Crochet chain cast-on
Make a crochet chain 4 stitches longer than the number of stitches you need to cast on. Pick up and knit stitches through back loops of the crochet chain (figure 1).

*Crochet cast-on
figure 1*

Pull out the crochet chain to expose live stitches when you're ready to knit in the opposite direction.

Crochet chain cast-on figure 2

Straight stitch: *Bring threaded needle out from back to front at base of the knitted stitch(es) you want to cover. Insert the needle at the top of the stitch(es) you want to cover. Repeat from *.

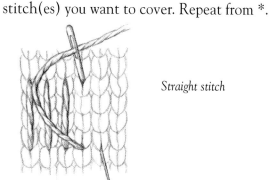

Straight stitch

Embroidery

Daisy stitch: Bring threaded needle out from back to front at the center of a knitted stitch. *Form a short loop and insert needle back where it came out. Keeping the loop under the needle, bring the needle back out in the center of the next stitch over.

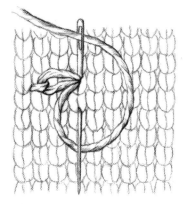

Daisy stitch

I-cord

With double-pointed needles, cast on desired number of stitches. *Without turning needle, slide the stitches to other end of the needle, pull the yarn around the back, and knit the stitches as usual; repeat from * for desired length. Follow the same procedure for purled I-cord, simply purling rather than knitting the stitches.

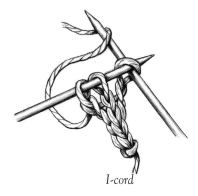

I-cord

Tops With a Twist

Kitchener stitch

This stitch is used to graft together two sets of live stitches. Thread a tapestry needle with the same yarn used for knitting. Place the needles holding the stitches paralell to each other and proceed as follows.

Step 1: Bring threaded needle through front stitch as if to purl and leave the stitch on the needle.

Step 2: Bring threaded needle through back stitch as if to knit and leave the stitch on the needle.

Step 3: Bring threaded needle through the same front stitch as if to knit and slip this stitch off the needle. Bring the threaded needle through the next front stitch as if to purl and leave the stitch on the needle.

Step 4: Bring threaded needle through the back stitch as if to purl, slip that stitch off, then bring the needle through the next back stitch as if to knit and leave this stitch on needle.

Repeat Steps 3 and 4 until no stitches remain.

M1 increase

With left needle tip, lift the strand between the last knitted stitch and the first stitch on the left needle, from front to back (figure 1). Knit the lifted loop through the back (figure 2).

M1 increase figure 1

M1 increase figure 2

Wrapping a stitch

Step 1: Work to turn point, slip next stitch purlwise to right needle. Bring yarn to front (figure 1).

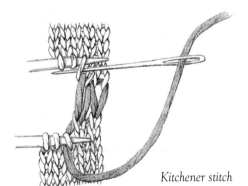

Kitchener stitch

Wrapping a stitch figure 1

Step 2: Slip the same stitch back to the left needle (wrapped stitch). Turn work and bring yarn in position for next stitch (figure 2).

Wrapping a stitch
figure 2

Yarn Butterfly

Make a butterfly by placing a tail of yarn in the palm of your left hand, end down towards the wrist, and clasping it with your last three fingers while holding your thumb and index finger out straight. With your right hand, wrap the yarn around your thumb and index finger in a figure-eight pattern. When the butterfly is the size you want, remove your fingers, hold the bundle in the middle, and wrap yarn firmly around the center several times. Cut the yarn, leaving a short tail. Twist a loop in the tail, wrap the yarn once around the bundle in the opposite direction, put the end through the loop, and pull it tight. The yarn will pull easily from the center of the butterfly beginning with the tail that was in the palm of your hand.

Yarn butterfly

Shaded Lattice Hat

Jeannine Bakriges
Brattleboro, Vermont

This hat was an unfortunate UFO (unfinished object) for a few years. It began with Cottage Creations's "Snakka du norsk—A Norwegian Winter Sports Cap" pattern. I had made mittens for a challenge sponsored by the Northeast Handspinners Association's "Gathering" and wanted a hat to match. The lattice pattern comes from 100 Landskapsvantar (ICA Kruiren, 1981). I used 100% handspun yarns, spun on either my Louet S10 or a Schacht Matchless.

The Cottage Creations hat has two layers of knitting around the ears, while my hat has three. . . very warm! In a nutshell, the hat begins at the light shaded edge, you work the lattice pattern, and continue with plain knitting for the lining. While the top is also knitted plain, the hat must be turned inside out first, then the knitting is reversed. The top is knitted firmly with a nine-point spiral of decreases. When you wear the hat, the smooth side on top is seen, and the knitted lining is smooth against your ears. Work a three-stitch purled I-cord on each edge of the color pattern. Pick up a third lining from the light I-cord and work down to the dark shading, then sew down. I knitted a Faeroese color pattern of kittens into the gray lining to commemorate Chloe, the new feline addition to our family. The kitten pattern comes from The Complete Book of Traditional Scandinavian Knitting *by Sheila McGregor (New York: St. Martin's Press, 1984).*

YARN: 100% handspun varieties of wool and wool blends including silk, mohair, alpaca, and angora. Cream (MC), light gray, medium gray, and dark gray. I used a lighter-weight yarn for the lining.

NEEDLES: Color pattern—size 4 (3.5 mm) 16" circular (cir); Linings—size 2 (2.75 mm) 16" cir; Top—size 3 (3.25 mm) 16" cir and double-pointed needles (dpn).

GAUGE: Varies from 13 to 15 sts = 2" (5 cm). Color pattern—6 ½ sts/in; Linings—7 ½ sts/in; top—7 sts/in.

With MC and color-pattern (largest) needle, CO 152 sts. Join, being careful not to twist sts. Place marker. Work Chart 1. Knit 3 rnds with dark gray. Change to lining (middle size) needle and lining yarn, and p1 rnd. Work in St st for 3 ¾" (9.5 cm). Break yarn. Turn piece inside out, change to top (smallest) needle and MC. Knit 1 rnd and inc 1 st—153 sts. Knit 4 rnds even, then work dec rnds as follows:

Rnd 1: *K15, k2tog; rep from *.

Rnd 2 and all even numbered rnds: Knit.

Rnd 3: *K14, k2tog; rep from *.

Continue in this manner, having 1 less st bet decs until 9 sts rem. Cut yarn leaving 6" (15-cm) tail. Using a tapestry needle, thread tail through the rem sts and tighten securely.

With RS facing and MC, work 3-st purl I-cord around cast-on edge. Kitchener st ends tog. With lining needle and lining yarn, pick up 154 sts

Tops With a Twist

along purl I-cord and work lining until 1 ¼" (3.2 cm) less than lattice-pattern piece. Work Chart 2, then work 3 rnds plain. Sew live sts down to first lining. With RS facing and darkest color, work 3-st I-cord along purl turning ridge. Kitchener st ends tog. I washed the hat in Eucalan and set it flat on towels to dry.

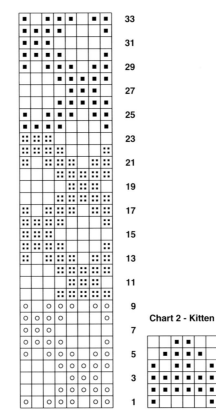

Chart 1 - Lattice

☐	cream (MC)
■	dark gray
∷	medium gray
○	light gray

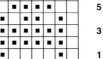

Chart 2 - Kitten

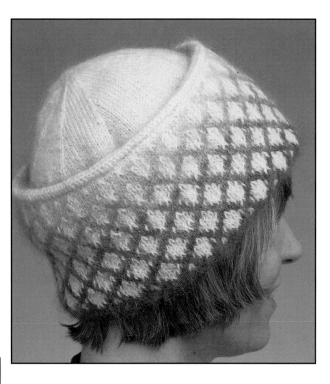

Big Mac Crochet Beret

Diane Ballerino
Supply, North Carolina

Almost half the fiber for this beret comes from a Japanese Akita. I used the dog's winter coat for the beret itself, and the summer coat for the band because the summer coat is softer and finer, also slightly lighter in color.

YARN: Handspun/handcarded Japanese Akita undercoat/Polworth and Icelandic wool/mohair blend (45% dog hair, 40% dark gray Polworth and black Icelandic undercoat, and 15% natural dark gray kid mohair). Yarn is 18 wraps/in, about 460 yds (420 meters), 5" spun singles, 2-ply.

NEEDLES: Steel crochet hook #2 (2.25 mm), or size to obtain gauge; I-cord—two size 1 (2.25 mm) double-pointed needles (dpn).

GAUGE: 15 sts and 15 rows = 2" (5 cm).

NOTIONS: Three red wooden "pony" beads.

Note: Work single crochet through both sides of stitch. Use the reverse side of sc as the right side of the hat.

Leaving a 20" (51 cm) tail, ch3, join with slip st to beginning ch st, forming a ring. Tuck the tail through center of ring; bundle into a yarn "butterfly" (to be used later to make the beret string).

Rnd 1: Ch1, then work 6sc in ring, end by sl st into ch-1—7 sts.

Rnd 2: Ch1, then inc 1 st in each st around, end by sl st into ch-1—14 sts.

Rnd 3: Ch1, inc 1 st in next st, *work 1sc, inc in next st; rep from * to end of rnd, end by sl st into ch-1; 7 increase "points"—21 sts.

Rnd 4: Ch1, inc 1 st in next st, *work 2sc, inc in next st; rep from * to end of rnd, end by sl st into ch-1—28 sts.

Rnd 5: Ch1, inc 1 st in next st, *work 3sc, inc in next st (making certain you inc 1 in same place as in prior row); rep from * to end of rnd, end by sl st into ch-1—35 sts.

Proceed in this manner working 1 more sc between increases on each rnd until you reach the desired diameter of hat. (This hat is 11 ¾" [30 cm] measured from one point to the flat area between points on the opposite edge.) Be sure new increases fall above first increase of previous rnd. This will make a subtle, curving spiral, and you should have 7 "points" on the hat (see schematic on page 22).

When you get to the desired diameter, work 3 plain rnds of sc (no inc), ending by sl st into ch-1 and ch1 to start next rnd. (In order to see the places to dec, place a safety pin at each "point" where you have inc—since the pattern may be slightly obliterated by the fuzziness of the yarn.)

After completing the 3rd plain rnd of sc, dec 1 st at each of the "points" (7 places) in each rnd, thereby dec 7 sts per rnd, until you reach

Tops With a Twist

desired head circumference, plus 1 ½" (3.8 cm) or so "ease" (in this hat, I proceeded for 2 ½" [6.5 cm]).

Band: Continue in sc in plain rnds, always ending sl st in 1st chain (this join will be the back of the band). Do this for 1" (2.5 cm) total. In order to make the openings for the cord, on the next rnd, ch1, 1sc, ch4, sk4, sc in next 5 sts, ch4, sk4, sc in each st as usual to end of rnd, end by sl st into ch-1. Ch1 to start next rnd, sc in each st and place 4sc sts in each of the ch4 areas (so that there is no change in the total number of sts) and proceed in straight rnds for another 1 ½" (3.8 cm). (You will have 2 rnds beyond the cord openings when you fold the band.) Break off when you have reached the end of the rnd.

I-cord: Using dpn, CO 4 sts, k4, *(do not turn) slide to opposite end of needle, k4; rep from * to desired length (41" [104 cm] in this hat). BO and tuck ends into ends of cord.

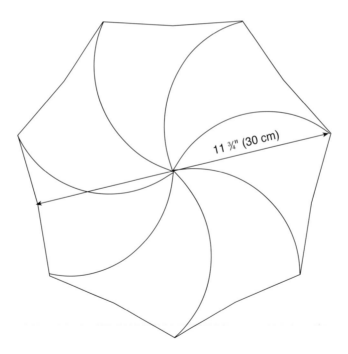

11 ¾" (30 cm)

Finishing: Fold band so that the reverse side of the sc is the right side and stitch in place. Thread cord through band, pulling ends through openings in band at back. Place both ends of the I-cord through one red pony bead (a "cinching bead"), then place each end of the I-cord through a pony bead and knot at each end.

Using the 20" (51-cm) tail at the beginning of the hat, pull up a loop, ch6, turn; sk first ch, sc in each st of chain—5 sts, turn; ch1, sc in each st; you have a small rectangle. With remaining tail, sew the long sides together. Thread remaining yarn down through the tube and secure. Weave in loose ends.

Circles with a Spark

Karen Bertino
Canandaigua, New York

This hat is topped with cascading circles crocheted with bullion stitch. A small amount of glitzy fiber provides the spark.

YARN: 3 oz. wool, mohair, and glitz blend from Fantom Farm (Massachusetts) spun fine for hat, a little thicker for circles.

NEEDLES: Size 7 (4.5 mm) 16" circular or size required to obtain gauge; size G (4.5 mm) crochet hook.

GAUGE: 10 sts and 14 rows = 2" (5 cm) in St st.

Stitches

Stockinette stitch (St st)
Knit every rnd.

Reverse stockinette stitch (rev St st)
Purl every rnd.

Cable rib stitch
Rnd 1: *P2, k2; rep from *.
Rnd 2 and 4: Knit the knits and purl the purls.
Rnd 3: *P2, knit 2nd st tbl, knit 1st st; rep from *.
Rep Rnds 1-4 for pattern.

CO 132 sts. Join, being careful not to twist sts. Place marker. Work cable pattern for 3 repeats.

Change to St st and work until piece measures 5 ½" (14 cm) from beg or to desired length. Work 2 rnds in rev St st to make a ridge. Work 2 rnds St st. Place sts on a holder (I use scrap yarn so that I can easily move and stretch the stitches). Make 15 bullion circles varying from 8 to 12 sts as described below. (I learned to do circles from Sylvia Cosh and James Walters at SOAR '97.)

Bullion circle
Make ring: Wind yarn clockwise around index finger, insert hook under the yarn. Yarn over and draw the yarn through (1 loop on hook), yo and draw the yarn through the loop.
Bullion ring: Work small circle as described above. Ch4, *wind yarn 8 to 12 times around shaft of hook, insert hook into ring, yo and draw through all the loops at once, yo and draw the yarn through loop on hook; rep from * 7 to 11 more

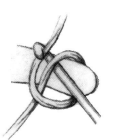

Wrap yarn clockwise around index finger and insert hook under the yarn.

Yarn over and draw the yarn through putting 1 loop on the hook, yo and draw the yarn through the loop.

Tops With a Twist

times. When finished, pull on yarn end to form small tight circle. Join with sl st in top of ch-4.

Sew circles together and to the hat sts held on waste yarn. I decided to put extras on, cascading them down the front, to show them off. If you choose to do this, the sts under the cascading circles must be bound off.

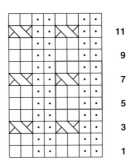

	purl
	knit 2nd st tbl; then knit first st
	pattern repeat

Wind yarn 8 to 12 times around hook, insert hook into ring, yo and draw yarn through all loops at once.

"Maybelline" Hat

Crik Christophel
Providence Forge, Virginia

I wanted a warm and colorful hat when I made this one, but didn't want to distort the color pattern by working decreases at the top. I did the obvious and just knitted a tube to desired length. I decided that dangling tassels were a perfect touch. This hat also makes a wonderful bag—great for gathering eggs.

YARN: 2-ply, bulky, handspun from "Maybelline," a border Leicester ewe. Dyed in the yarn with natural dyes.

A = Logwood dyed @ 50% WOG (weight of goods) with premordant of alum 10% WOG, tartaric acid 5% WOG.

B = Marigold (dried flowerheads) dyed @ 300% WOG with premordant of alum 10% WOG, tartaric acid 5% WOG.

C = Cochineal dyed @ 30% WOG with tartaric acid 15% WOG.

D = Cochineal dyed 1st exhaust from dyepot of 30% WOG with tartaric acid 15% WOG and tin .5% WOG.

NEEDLES: Sizes 8 (5 mm) and 9 (5.5 mm) 16" circular or double-pointed (dpn).

GAUGE: 8 sts and 9 ½ rows = 2" (5 cm) over color knitting.

Stitches

Braid stitch

Rnd 1: *K1 A, k1 D; rep from * to marker. Bring yarns to the front between the points of the needles, pull out 2 or 3 yards of each yarn.

Rnd 2: *P1 A, drop A, bring D *over* A and p1 D, drop D, bring A *over* D; rep from * to marker. Yarns will twist on themselves during this rnd but will untwist on following rnd.

Rnd 3: *P1 A, drop A, bring D *under* A and p1 D, drop D, bring A *under* D; rep from * to marker. Cut D.

With A, and smaller needle, CO 78 sts. Join, being careful not to twist sts. Place marker.
Note: Center back of hat is the "seam."
Work braid stitch with colors A and D. Follow chart to end. Divide sts evenly onto two dpn and Kitchener st tog.

Tassels: (from *Finishes in the Ethnic Tradition* by Suzanne Baizerman and Karen Searle [St. Paul: Dos Tejedoras, 1978]). Wrap desired amount of Color C around cardboard of desired length. Place a long length of yarn of Color A between wrapped yarn and cardboard at one end and tie firmly. Cut yarn bundle at other end. Wrap tassel with color B 7 times about 1" (2.5 cm) from tied end, and secure ends of color B. Crochet the 2 strands of Color A into a chain of desired length and fasten off, leaving enough yarn for tying to hat points. Attach tassels to points by pulling yarns through to inside with a crochet hook and tying into a firm bow. Remove tassels when washing hat.

Maybelline

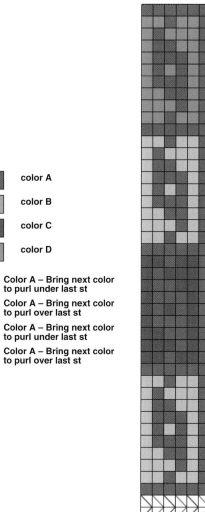

color A

color B

color C

color D

⟍ Color A – Bring next color to purl under last st

⟋ Color A – Bring next color to purl over last st

⟍ Color A – Bring next color to purl under last st

⟋ Color A – Bring next color to purl over last st

Acorn Hat

Lauri Copeland
Overland Park, Kansas

While spinning and planning for this project I knew that in spite of the Kansas City heat and humidity, it would soon be fall. Finally.

I began with 4 oz. of red superwash merino roving from Ashland Bay. The resulting 3-ply yarn measures 400 yds/lb., (using McMorran Balance). Based on this measurement, I used about 110 yds for the main body. I was glad to have extra handspun—I started over several times. Somewhere a voice kept reminding me that "This wouldn't happen if you checked your gauge before beginning." Designing as I knitted also contributed to these "do-overs." I knew I wanted a somewhat simple hat so that I could play with the placement of the crocheted acorns and leaves. The braid stitch trim is worth the extra effort and the ribbing of band stitch (often used as a heel stitch for socks) adds a little more stability to the hat base. Have fun!

YARN: Ashland Bay Superwash merino approximately 2.5 oz (MC), 2-ply scraps of wool for acorns, leaves, and braid stitch trim (CC).

NEEDLES: Sizes 2 (2.75 mm) & 3 (3.25 mm) 16" circular needle and/or double pointed needles (dpn); size B (2.0 mm) crochet hook.

GAUGE: 10 sts = 2" (5 cm) in St st on larger needle.

Stitches
Braid stitch
Rnd 1: *K1 MC, k1 CC; rep from *. Bring yarns to the front between the points of the needles, pull out 2 or 3 yards of each yarn.

Rnd 2: *P1 MC, drop MC, bring CC *over* MC and p1 CC, drop CC, bring MC *over* CC; rep from *. Yarns will twist on themselves during this rnd but will untwist on following rnd.

Rnd 3: *P1 MC, drop MC, bring CC *under* MC and p1 CC, drop CC, bring MC *under* CC; rep from *. Cut CC.

Band stitch
Rnd 1: *K1, sl 1 wyb; rep from *.
Rnd 2: K1 rnd. Rep these two rnds for pattern.

With MC and smaller needles, CO 96 sts. Join, being careful not to twist sts. Place marker. Knit 1 rnd. Work 3 rnds braid stitch. Change to larger needles and knit 1 rnd MC. Work band stitch until piece measures 2 ½" (6.5 cm) or desired length of band, ending with Rnd 2 at marker. Change to smaller needles. Work 3 rnds braid stitch.

Main body: Change to larger needles. Knit 1 rnd inc evenly to 132 sts. Knit 4 rnds even.

Decrease rnd: *K1, k2tog, k17, ssk; rep from * to marker. Knit 3 rnds even.

Next decrease rnd: *K1, k2tog, k15, ssk; repeat from * to marker.

Tops With a Twist

Knit 3 rnds even. Continue in this manner dec 2 sts in each section (12 sts per rnd) every fourth rnd until 24 sts rem, changing to dpn when necessary.

Top: Knit 12 rnds even on these 24 sts. *K2 tog; rep from *, cut yarn, thread tail through rem 12 sts pulling tight to close hole at top.

Crochet acorns and leaves: Use scraps of hand-spun in colors of choice and appropriate size crochet hook.

Acorn

Outside of acorn: Leaving a 4" (10-cm) tail, ch6 and join to form ring. Dc in center 12 times and join. Sc in each dc and join. Sc 3 rnds, sl st one rnd and join. Cut yarn. Weave in tail and turn up to form small ridge at open end. *Center of acorn:* Using lighter color, ch5 and join—dc in center 10 times and join. Sc 3 rnds and join. Cut leaving a 2" (5-cm) tail, close up opening with tail, and pull center of acorn through inside opening of outside of acorn.

Leaves

Row 1: Ch4, sk 1, sc in next 3 sts, ch3, turn.
Row 2: Sk 1 ch, sl st in next 2 ch, 2 sc in each of next 3 sc, ch3, turn.
Row 3: Sk 1 ch, sl st in next 2 ch, sc in next 5 sc, ch3, turn.
Row 4: Sk 1 ch, sl st in next 2 ch, sc in next 4 sc, ch3, turn.
Row 5: Sk 1 ch, sl st in next 2 ch, sc in next 3 sc, ch3, turn.
Row 6: Sk 1 ch, sl st in next 2 ch, sc in next 2 sc, ch3, turn.
Row 7: Sk 1 ch, sl st in next 2 ch, sc in next sc, ch1, turn, sl st, finish off.

Finishing: I blocked the hat with steam and a rolled-up towel. Feel free to make several acorns and leaves and experiment with placement.

Rainbow Lambs' Tails Cap

Lynn Cosell
Pearisburg, Virginia

I decided to make this hat during lambing last spring. I used a single rainbow dye pot (blue, turquoise, red, and yellow) for reasons of time. I separated the resulting locks into three groups: saturated colors, light unsaturated colors, and dark unsaturated colors. I stripped the first group through a cotton card and spun from the individual locks for maximum color variation. I combed the latter two groups together, using equal numbers of locks from both groups to obtain the background yarn. Both yarns were Navajo three-plied. Throughout the hat, I used the yarns as follows: three rounds of background (dark), one round of bright.

The lambs' tails are from Barbara G. Walker's A Second Treasury of Knitting Patterns (Pittsville, Wisconsin: Schoolhouse Press, 1998). Because I wanted to knit the cap from the top of the crown down, I purled the tails instead of knitting them, to help them lie in the right direction. I found purled tails easier to work than Walker's version, because the right-hand needle does not have to be removed and reinserted while casting on.

The cap is self-lined for warmth. It is knitted from the top of the outer crown and ending with the top of the inside crown.

YARN: Rainbow-dyed dark and bright superfine Merino wool from Sonata, a four-year-old ewe.

5 ½ oz. of 3-ply yarn at 28 wraps per inch.

NEEDLES: Size 0 (2 mm) double-pointed needles (dpn) set of 4.

GAUGE: 24 sts and 28 rows = 2" (5cm) over k1, p1 ribbing.

Stitches

Lambs' Tail stitch (LT): P1 st, and place it on left-hand needle but do not remove right-hand needle from the just-made stitch. Repeat three times, having 4 new stitches on left-hand needle. Purl first two of these normally, transferring to right-hand needle, then pass first of these stitches over the second, binding off one stitch. Purl and bind off 3 more stitches.

Note: Work all lambs' tail rounds with bright.

Top of hat: Using dark, CO 6 sts, divide on three dpn. Join, being careful not to twist sts. Place marker for beg of rnd.

Rnd 1: Knit.

Rnd 2: [K1, M1] 6 times—12 sts.

Rnds 3 and 5: Knit.

Rnd 4: [K1, M1, k1] 6 times—18 sts.

Rnd 6: [K1, M1, k1, M1, k1, place marker] 5 times, k1, M1, k1, M1, k1—30 sts.

Rnd 7: Using bright, *k1, p1, LT, p1, k1; rep from *.

Rnd 8: Using dark, *k1, M1 [p1, k1] to 2 sts before m, p1, M1, k1; rep from *—42 sts.

Rnd 9: *K2, p1, [k1, p1] to 2 sts before m, k2; rep from *.

Rnd 10: *K1, M1, [k1, p1] to 2 sts before m, k1, M1, k1; rep from *—54 sts.

Rnd 11: Using bright, *k1, p1, LT, [p1, k1, p1, LT] to 2 sts before m, p1, k1; rep from *.

Repeat rounds 8-11 inc as established, until you reach desired circumference. End on Rnd 11. Each of the six sections should have a multiple of 4 sts plus 1.

Next rnd: With dark, k1, [p1, k1] to m, M1; rep from *. There is a multiple of 4 sts plus 2 between markers.

Next rnd: *[K1, p1] to m, k2; rep from *.

Next rnd: *M1, [k1, p1] to 2 sts before m, k1, M1, k1; rep from *. There is a multiple of four sts between markers. Remove all but the beg of rnd marker.

Work Crown:

Rnd 1: With bright, *p1, LT, p1, k1; rep from *.

Rnds 2, 3, and 4: With dark, *p1, k1; rep from *.

Rnd 5: With bright, *p1, k1, p1, LT; rep from *.

Rnds 6, 7, and 8: With dark, *p1, k1; rep from *.

Repeat last 8 rounds until hat is desired length less desired width of brim. Continuing with 3 rnds dark, 1 rnd bright, work even in (p1, k1), no lambs' tails, for about 2 ¼" (5.5 cm) or desired length.

Next rnd (make crease): *K2tog; rep from * to marker.

Next rnd: *K1, M1; rep from * to marker. Continue in k1, p1 ribbing until brim is 4 ¼" (11 cm) or desired length

Next rnd (make fold): *P2tog; rep from * to marker.

Next rnd: *K1, M1; rep from * to marker.

Continue in k1, p1 ribbing for outside of brim and then lining, reversing original shaping for inner crown.

Weave in tail of yarn, then push in inner crown center to meet outer crown center. Fold up brim.

Turkish Braid Hat

Susan Crawford
Cedar Glen, California

This hat uses a series of braid stitches to form a nice firm hatband. The braid stitch pattern is followed by seed stitch.

YARN: 6 oz. of main yarn and about ½ oz. each of two other, highly contrasting yarns.

NEEDLES: Size 8, 16" circular (cir) and double-pointed (dpn).

GAUGE: Determine gauge, CO enough sts to equal the circumference of your head less ½ inch. (Ex: 21"[53 cm] circumference–½ in [1.3 cm]) x 5 sts per in (2 sts per cm) = 103 sts.

Stitches
Seed stitch
Rnd 1: *K1, p1; rep from * to marker.
Rnd 2: Purl the knits and knit the purls.

Braid stitch
Rnd 1: *K1 MC, k1 CC; rep from to marker. Bring yarns to the front between the points of the needles, pull out 2 or 3 yards of each yarn.
Rnd 2: *P1 MC, drop MC, bring CC over MC and p1 CC, drop CC, bring MC over CC; rep from * to marker. Yarns will twist on themselves during this rnd but will untwist on following rnd.
Rnd 3: *P1 MC, drop MC, bring CC under MC and p1 CC, drop CC, bring MC under CC; rep from * to marker. Cut CC, change to larger needles and k1 row MC.

With MC, CO 104 sts. Join, being careful not to twist sts. Place marker.

Brim: Knit St st for 4" (10 cm).
Change to CC. Knit 5 or 6 sequences of braid stitch to create hatband about 2 ½" (6.5 cm).
Knit 1 rnd with MC dec 1 st—103 sts.
Work in seed stitch for 1 1/2" (3.8 cm) inc 1 st on last rnd—104 sts.

Begin crown decreases:
Rnd 1: *Sl 1, k2tog, psso, k10; rep from *.
Rnds 2, 3, and 4: Knit.
Rnd 5: *Sl 1, k2tog, psso, k8; rep from *.
Rnds 6, 7, and 8: Knit.
Continue dec in this manner until 8 sts rem.
Next rnd: [K2tog] 4 times.
Knit the rem 4 sts for ½" (1.3 cm). Tie off by running the end of the yarn through the rem sts. Make a knot and leave a little end sticking up.

Tops With a Twist

Beaded Wonder

Carolyn Doe
Kootenai, Idaho

The pattern for this hat started from a project in Knitter's magazine (#36, Fall 1994) that was focused on African designs. I started with the headband and straight needles, connecting at the seam to make a circle. Then I picked up with white around the circumference and knitted up the inside of the band. I then connected the edges on the next round and continued on up to make the top of the hat. I substituted some of my own designs in the pattern. When I ran out of colored yarn, I couldn't complete the top as planned, so I stuck it on my head and played with what I had until I found a shape that looked good to me. I added tucks, sewed the top flap down, and embellished with buttons and beads.

YARN: I spun the yarn on my drop spindle. The white 2-ply (MC) was from an unknown roving I traded for. The colored 2-ply (CC) came from bits of brightly dyed Lincoln leftover from a friend's workshop ages ago. I washed the bits and placed them in a basket, grabbing different colors as I spun. Really fun and colorful!

NEEDLES: It has been over a year's worth of knitting since I made this. I'll guess I used size 4 (3.5 mm), 16" circular (cir) and double-pointed (dpn), size F (3.75 mm) crochet hook.

GAUGE: Varies from 14 sts = 2" (5 cm) for headband to 12 sts = 2" (5 cm) for top.

NOTIONS: Waste yarn, 3 buttons, glass beads.

Band: With waste yarn, crochet hook, and circular needle, crochet CO 21 sts. Work pin stripe, (k1 MC, k1 CC), across the 21 sts. Maintaining pin stripe, work back and forth in St st for 22" (56 cm). Remove waste yarn, join beginning to end with Kitchener st.

With MC and cir needle, knit up 102 sts along one edge of band. Join. Place marker. Purl one rnd. Knit to the width of the band, join to other edge of band by knitting the needle sts tog with the sts along the edge of the band, thereby making the band a double thickness.

Top: Follow chart through rnd 43.

Beg dec rnds: *Ssk, work in pattern to last 2 sts before marker, k2tog; rep from * every rnd 17 times-64 sts rem. Continue to end of chart. Divide sts evenly onto two dpn and Kitchener st tog.

Finishing: Fold top down at side and stitch in place. Insert two tucks in material above band and stitch in place. Sew on 3 buttons at edge of fold. String multiple baubles and beads and stitch below fold.

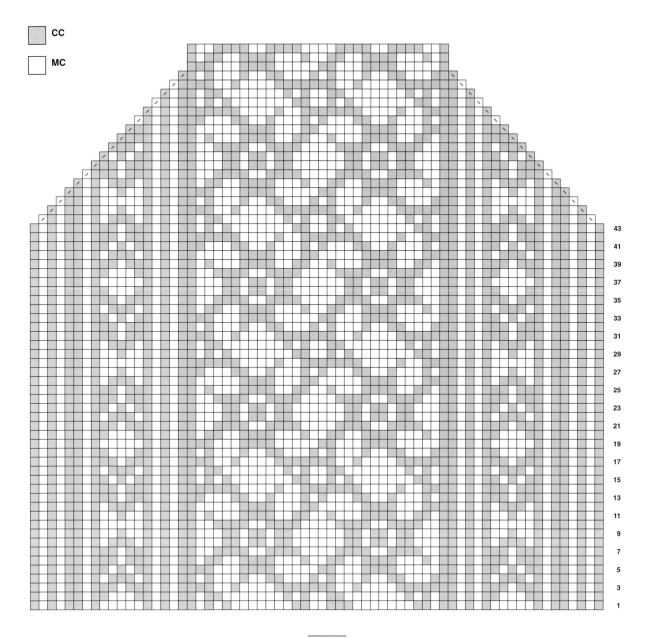

Bon-Bon Bowler

Susan Z. Douglas
Topsham, Maine

Is it confectionery or millinery? This hat reminds me of white chocolate candy. Knit it sideways using short rows and graft the last row carefully to the first, minding the stitch patterns. The reward is a hat that can't be put on backwards, and that looks good enough to eat!

YARN: About 5 oz. 2-ply heavy worsted-weight handspun, approximately 10 wraps per inch. (I spun my domestic wool top from Halcyon Yarn on my drop-spindle).

NEEDLES: Straight knitting needles size 10 (6 mm) or size needed to obtain gauge.

GAUGE: 7 sts and 14 row = 2" (5 cm) in garter stitch.

NOTIONS: Polyester stuffing; cable needle (cn); small bit of waste yarn.

Note: I felted my finished hat slightly. You might like to try a gauge of 4 sts/inch without felting.

Stitches
2/2 Left Cross (2/2LC)
S1 2 to (cn), hold to front, k2, k2 from cn.
2/2 Left Purl Cross (2/2 LPC)
S1 2 to cn, hold to front, p2, k2 from cn.
2/2 Right Purl Cross (2/2 RPC)
S1 2 to cn, hold to back, k2, p2 from cn.

2/2 Right Rib Cross (2/2 RRC)
S1 2 to cn, hold to back, k2, p1, k1 from cn.

Wrap and turn
Wyb, s1 1 st, bring yarn to front, place s1 st back onto left needle, turn work to continue.

Using waste yarn, chain cast-on as follows: Crochet a chain of waste yarn. In the back bumps of the chain, pick up 46 sts (counts as first row).

Row 2: (WS): K10, (p1, k1) 4 times, p2, k4, p2, k14, wrap and turn—40 sts worked.

Row 3: K16, p4, k2, (p1, k1) 4 times, p10.

Row 4: K10, (p1, k1) 4 times, p2, k4, p2, k12, wrap and turn—38 sts worked.

Row 5: K12, 2/2 LC, p2, 2/2LPC, (p1, k1) 3 times, p10.

Row 6: K10, (p1, k1) 3 times, p2, k4, p2, k12, wrap and turn—36 sts worked.

Row 7: K12, 2/2 LC, p2, 2/2 LPC, (p1, k1) 2 times, p10.

Row 8: K10, (p1, k1) 2 times, p2, k4, p2, k12, wrap and turn—34 sts worked.

Row 9: K12, 2/2LC, p2, 2/2 LPC, p1, k1, p10

Row 10: K10, p1, k1, p2, k4, p2, k12, wrap and turn—32 sts worked.

Row 11: K14, p4, k2, p1, k1, p10.

Row 12: K10, p1, k1, p2, k4, p2, k10, wrap and turn—30 sts worked.

Row 13: K12, p4, k2, p1, k1, p10.

Row 14: K10, p1, k1, p2, k4, p2, k9, wrap and turn—29 sts worked.

Row 15: K11, p4, k2, p1, k1, p10.

Row 16: K10, p1, k1, p2, k4, p2, k11, wrap and turn—31 sts worked.

Row 17: K13, p4, k2, p1, k1, p10.

Row 18: K10, p1, k1, p2, k4, p2, k13, wrap and turn—33 sts worked.

Row 19: K11, 2/2 RPC, p2, 2/2 RRC, p1, k1, p10.

Row 20: K10, (p1, k1) 2 times, p2, k4, p2, k13, wrap and turn—35 sts worked.

Row 21: K11, 2/2 RPC, p2, 2/2 RRC, (p1, k1) 2 times, p10.

Row 22: K10, (p1, k1) 3 times, p2, k4, p2, k13, wrap and turn—37 sts worked.

Row 23: K11, 2/2 RPC, p2, 2/2 RRC, (p1, k1) 3 times, p10.

Row 24:<P> K10, (p1, k1) 4 times, p2, k4, p2, k13, wrap and turn—39 sts worked.

Row 25: K15, p4, k2, (p1, k1) 4 times, p10.

Row 26: K10, (p1, k1) 4 times, p2, k4, p2, k15, wrap and turn—41 sts worked.

Row 27: K17, p4, k2, (p1, k1) 4 times, p10.

Row 28: K10, (p1, k1) 4 times, p2, k4, p2, k20—46 sts worked.

Row 29: K22, p4, k2, (p1, k1) 4 times, p10.

Rep rows 2 through 29 three times, then work rows 2 through 28 once.

Finishing: Graft the first row to the last. Since both of these rows face the same direction, the stitch patterns should match. I had to experiment a bit to figure out where the yarn had to enter and exit the stitches. Roll the brim to the outside, stuff, and sew in place with loose sts, retaining the elasticity. Weave in loose ends. I wet the finished hat, squeezed out the excess water, and popped it into a hot dryer. When it was the desired size and almost dry, I shaped it on a form made from rolled-up hand towels and washcloths.

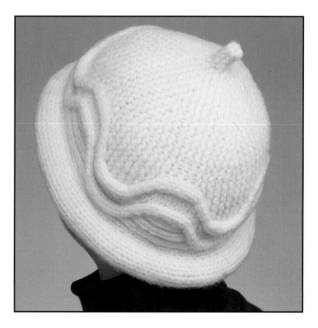

Jewels

Verna Friedrichsen
Wilton, Connecticut

These whimsical little hats not only make a unique piece of jewelry, they'd look terrific hanging from a Christmas tree or used to adorn gift packages.

YARN: Very fine, fingering type, leftovers of merino, cormo silk, and alpaca.
NEEDLES: Size 1 double pointed set of 4.
GAUGE: 8–9 sts = 1" (2.5 cm).

CO about 30 sts adjusting the number for any pattern repeat you plan to use. Divide sts onto 3 needles and join, being careful not to twist sts. Place marker.

Round-top ski hat: K1, p1 for one rnd. Knit 6 rnds, centering any chosen color pattern. P1 rnd for the fold. Knit 3 rnds. Change direction of knitting by: Sl 1, bring yarn forward of work between needles, sl the same st back to left needle. Turn your work inside out and begin knitting in opposite direction. Knit in St st for ½–1" (1.3–2.5 cm) depending on style of hat. Dec 6 sts every other rnd by hiding them in the pattern or by stacking them to form ridges. End off. Add pom-pom or tassel or leave plain.

Square-top ski hat: Work in St st for 3" (7.5 cm). Divide sts evenly onto two dpn and Kitchener st tog. Turn 1" (2.5 cm) at bottom to inside and sew down. Turn inside out and fold the two corners at top of hat at a 45° angle and tie tog.

Peruvian: *Earflaps (make 2):* With tan, CO 1 st. Inc 1 in that st. Work St st, inc 1 st at beg of each knit row until you have 5 sts. Break yarn. For second earflap, inc 1 st at end of each row until you have 5 sts.
On a separate needle, CO 5 sts. Knit 5 sts from one earflap. CO 10 sts, k5 sts from second earflap, CO 5 sts. Join being careful not to twist sts. Knit 3 rnds. Work Alpaca chart. Finish off. Make tassel on each earflap.

Tam-O-Shanter: CO 30 sts. Work k1, p1 rib for 3 rnds.
Inc Rnd: Inc 1 st in each st around—60 sts.
Knit 7 rnds.
Dec Rnd: *K2tog, k8; rep from *—54 sts.
Rep dec rnd 8 more times working 1 less st between decreases on each rnd—6 sts rem. Cut yarn leaving a 6" (15-cm) tail. With tapestry needle, thread end through rem sts. Fasten securely.
Thread finished hats onto a crocheted chain of necklace length.

Tops With a Twist

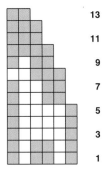

Alpaca chart

13
11
9
7
5
3
1

Pearls Squared

Verna Friedrichsen
Wilton, Connecticut

This colorful checkerboard hat is very simple to knit. And there's no limit to the variations in color. Do your thing!

YARN: 3 oz sport weight handspun Corriedale and Merino in various colors.
NEEDLES: Size 3 (3.25 mm), 16" circular needle
GAUGE: 12 sts and 16 rows = 2" (5 cm) over garter st.

Pattern stitch

Use one light color (A) and one dark color (B) for each 3-rnd pattern.
Rnd 1: *K2 color A, k2 color B; rep from *.
Rnd 2: *P2 color A, p2 color B; rep from *.
Rnd 3: *P2 color A, p2 color B; rep from *.
Repeat these 3 rnds for pattern. As you progress, change one or both colors at Rnd 1. The pattern will accommodate small differences in yarn weights.

With A, CO 120 sts, (or other multiple of 4 for different size). Join being careful not to twist sts.

Place marker. Purl 2 rows. Work 4" (10 cm) in pattern. On the next Rnd 1 of pattern change the direction of knitting by removing marker, sl 1 st, bring yarn forward between the two needles, sl the same st back to the left needle, replace marker. Turn work inside out and begin knitting Rnd 1 of pattern in opposite direction. Continue until hat measures 10" (25.5 cm) from beginning. End with Rnd 3.

Decrease for crown: Keeping in 3-rnd color pattern as established, work decreases as follows:
Rnd 1: *K2tog, k6; rep from *—105 sts.
Rnds 2, 3, 5, 6, 8, and 9: Work even in pattern.
Rnd 4: K3, *k2tog, k5; rep from * end k2—90 sts.
Rnd 7: *K2tog, k1; rep from *—60 sts.
Rnd 10: *K2tog; rep from *—30 sts.

Finishing: Thread yarn through rem sts. Tie off and weave in loose ends.

Make 3 braids, each from a different yarn, 10" (25.5-cm) long, leaving several inches of free yarn at each end. Knot them all together at one end leaving yarn free. Knot them separately at the other ends. Attach large knot to hat with free yarn.

Turkish Infant Cap

Lisa Gwinner
Rochester, New York

I used 11" circular needles for the body of the hat and double-pointed needles (dpn) to decrease for the crown. You'll also need a circular needle two sizes smaller for ribbing. For fingering to sportweight wool, try size 2 needles to achieve gauge, working up or down a couple of sizes as necessary.

YARN: All handspun, light blue indigo-dyed Corriedale and dark blue indigo overdyed gray Romney. Spin 2-ply, approximately sport weight.

NEEDLES: Body—Size 2 (2.75 mm) 11" circular needle and double-pointed needles; Ribbing—Size 0 (2 mm) 11" circular.

GAUGE: 18 sts = 2" (5 cm) measured over color pattern.

CO 124 sts with smaller needle. Join, being careful not to twist sts. Work k2, p2 ribbing for 7 rnds. Change to St st and larger needle and work 1 rnd, inc 2 sts—126 sts.

Begin color pattern following chart. Work first 25 rnds of chart. Change to dpn on next plain rnd, placing 42 sts (2 decrease panels) on each of 3 needles. Follow decreases as charted. First dec rnd is worked as follows: *K1, k2tog, k16 in pat-tern, ssk; rep from *. There will be 18 sts when chart is completed. K2tog around—9 sts. For topknot, work around on 9 sts for 3"–4" (7.5–10 cm). Cut wool, leaving 6" (15-cm) tail. Thread tail onto tapestry needle and gather rem sts onto tail. Tighten and fasten off. Weave all tails to the inside of the cap. Tie knot in topknot.

I strongly recommend soaking all infant garments to eliminate excess dye. I just wash as usual, but leave garments in the soapy and rinse baths longer to get as much dye out as possible. I did not block this hat, just laid it flat to dry.

Turkish Infant Cap

light

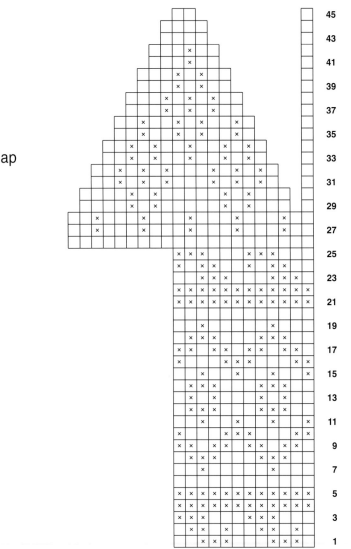
dark

Twisted Tail Top

Tops With a Twist

Jean Inda
Eugene, Oregon

A simple little corkscrew makes a fanciful statement about this otherwise unadorned hat.

YARN: Bulky Romney, approximately 4 oz.
NEEDLES: Size 6 (4 mm) circular and double-pointed needles (dpn)
GAUGE: 8 sts = 2" (5 cm) over St st.
NOTIONS: Florist wire.

Using a bulky yarn and circular needle, CO 80 sts. Join being careful not to twist sts. Place marker. Knit until hat measures 7" (18 cm) or desired length.

Begin decreases as follows, changing to dpn when the sts will no longer fit on circular needle.

Rnd 1: *K6, k2tog; rep from * to marker—70 sts.
Rnd 2 and all even rnds: Knit.
Rnd 3: *K5, k2tog; rep from * to marker—60 sts.
Rnd 5: *K4, k2tog; rep from * to marker—50 sts.
Rnd 7: *K3, k2tog; rep from * to marker—40 sts.
Rnd 9: *K2, k2tog; rep from * to marker—30 sts.
Rnd 11: *K1, k2tog; rep from * to marker—20 sts.
Rnd 13: *K2tog; rep from * to marker—10 sts.
Rnd 14: *K2tog; rep from *—5 sts.

Use rem 5 sts to make an I-cord about 8" (20.5 cm) long. Break yarn and draw through the rem sts. Fasten off and run end down into cord. Weave in any remaining tails.

I lightly felted some fiber around a doubled piece of florist wire. I inserted it into the cord and secured it at the top of the hat. I then shaped the tail into a twist.

Fair Isle Tam

Sarah Miller, Knitter
Livermore, Maine
Leah O'Donnell, Spinner
Canaan, Maine

Tams are timeless, and here we offer one with a fairly simple Fair Isle pattern. Experiment with your favorite colors and motifs.

YARN: 50:50 blend of wool and angora; about 160 yds or 2–3 oz, 2 ply, sportweight, 12 wraps per inch. MC oxford, 1.5 oz; CC1 light gray, ¼ oz.; CC2 white, ¼ oz.

NEEDLES: 16" circular needle sizes 6 (4 mm) and 7 (4.5 mm), dpn size 7 (4.5 mm).

GAUGE: 12 sts and 13 rows = 2" (5 cm) over St st.

Stitches
Knit-Slip Stitch
Rnd 1: *K1, wyf, sl 1, wyb; rep from *.
Rnd 2: *Wyf, sl 1, wyb, k1; rep from *.

With MC and smaller cir needle, CO 92 sts. Join being careful not to twist sts. Place marker.

Band
Rnds 1–3: Work Knit-Slip Stitch.
Rnds 4–10: Work Chart 1 (band).
Rnds 11–13: With MC work Knit-Slip Stitch.

Body
Change to larger needle.
Rnd 1: *K2, M1; rep from * to marker—138 sts.
Rnd 2: Knit.
Rnd 3: [K4, M1, k5, M1] 15 times, end k3—168 sts. Work Chart 2 through row 24.
Rnd 25: With MC, ([k2, k2tog] 5 times, k1) 8 times—128 sts rem.

Continue with Chart 2 and work decreases until 8 sts rem, changing to dpn when necessary. Cut yarn leaving a 6" (15-cm) tail. With tapestry needle, thread end through rem sts. Fasten securely. Weave in loose ends. Block over large (10 ½"–11" [26.5–28 cm]) dinner plate.

Tops With a Twist

Tam Chart 2 - body

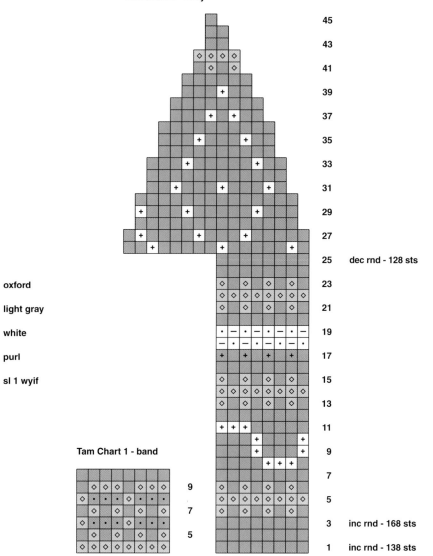

Tam Chart 1 - band

Highway Woman's Hat

Selma Miriam
Westport, Connecticut

Telephone cable wire is the perfect thing for taming the floppy brim on this hat. Small amounts of raspberry silk complement the subtle heather wool.

YARN: Heather wool with a little silk, 3-ply sportweight, 3 ½ oz. (MC); small amount raspberry silk (CC).

NEEDLES: Size 3, (3.25 mm) 16" circular and double-pointed needles (dpn); Size 2 (2.75 mm), 16" circular.

GAUGE: 10 sts = 2" (5 cm) on larger needle over pattern.

NOTIONS: Tapestry needle, telephone cable wire.

With MC and smaller cir needle, CO 96 sts. Join being careful not to twist sts. Place marker.

Rnd 1: Knit.

Rnds 2 & 3: Purl.

Rnd 4: Change to larger needle and knit.

Make hatband: With CC, work Chart 1. Break yarn. With MC knit 1 rnd, purl 2 rnds, and knit 1 rnd.

Crown: Follow chart.

Top: Follow chart.

Break yarn and use tapestry needle to run through rem sts.

Brim: With MC, pick up 96 sts around cast-on edge.

Rnd 1: Knit.

Rnd 2: *K8, M1; rep from *—108 sts.

Rnd 3: *M1, k7, M1, p2; rep from *—132 sts.

Rnd 4: *K8, p3; rep from *.

Rnd 5: *M1, k7, M1, p4; rep from *—156 sts

Rnd 6: *K8, p5; rep from *.

Rnd 7: *M1, k7, M1, p6; rep from *—180 sts.

Note: On rnds without incs there will always be 8 knit sts between purl sts.

When there are 17 purl sts in each section, stop increases—300 sts. Work 3 or 4 more rnds if desired, working sts as they appear.

Finishing: Knit 1 rnd, purl 2 rnds, bind off with CC using knit sts.

With CC, sew 2 strands of thin, colored telephone cable wire into the reverse stocking st edge of brim. Twist edges of wire together making a loop at each end. Wrap well with yarn. Gather brim st onto wire to suit your taste.

Finally, make a ball top out of contrasting yarn. CO 8 sts on dpns. Join being careful not to twist sts. Join being careful not to twist sts.

Rnd 1: Knit

Rnd 2: *M1, k2; rep from *.

Rnd 3: Knit.

Rnd 4: *M1, k1; rep from *—24 sts.

Rnds 5 and 6: Knit.

Tops With a Twist

Make a little ball of scrap yarn and stuff it into the little pouch you are knitting.

Rnd 8: *K2tog; rep from *—6 sts.

Cut yarn, leaving a tail and sew up rem sts. Sew firmly to center top of hat.

Chart 2 - crown

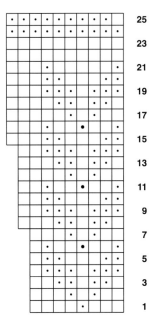

Chart 3 - top

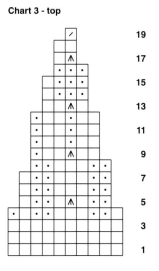

Chart 1 - hatband

Work with CC

	main color
	purl
	k2tog
	dbl dec: sl 2tog k-wise, k1, p2sso
	bobble: [k1, p1] 2 times in same st; pass last 3 sts over first st

Fool's Hat

Hazel Murray
Victoria, British Columbia

After I got the idea for the hat, I looked around for some basic patterns to use. At this time I did not know you were offering a contest, or I would have been more original. I have to give credit to Anna Zil-boorg's Fine & Fanciful Hats to Knit (Asheville, North Carolina: Lark Books, 1997) for the black design. I used it because the number of stitches in the repeat divided into the number of stitches I needed for the band, i.e. 19 x 6 = 114 sts. This number was determined by the thickness of my yarn. Just in case I guessed wrong, I left a slit in the double-thick band to insert elastic, if needed.

I'd spun most of the yarn previously, but the lovely shaded yarn in two of the points came from a little bag of roving given to me by Anne Field-and it's perfect here.

I separated the blue/red shades from the yellow/green shades, spinning them into separate plies. I plied the blue/reds with gray and the yellow/green with beige. (If I had to do it over again I would have created three colors, but I committed the sin of not planning ahead. Doesn't everyone?)

I don't know if I have the courage to wear this hat, but I have two granddaughters who would kill for it.

YARN: Odds and ends of handspun in various colors (C) plus black (A) and white (B)— total 120 grams (4+ oz.).

NEEDLES: 2.5 mm, 16" circular and double-pointed (dpn).

GAUGE: 14 sts and 19 rows = 2" (5 cm) over St st.

Facing: With A and circular needle, CO 114 sts. Join being careful not to twist sts. Place marker. Knit 1 rnd, cut yarn. With C, work in St st for 1" (2.5 cm). Join A and B and work braid as follows:

Rnd 1: *K1 A, k1 B; rep from * to marker. Bring yarns to the front between the points of the needles and pull out 2 or 3 yards of each yarn.

Rnd 2: *P1 A, drop A, bring B *over* A and p1 B, drop B, bring A *over* B; rep from * to marker. Yarns will twist on themselves during this rnd but will untwist on following rnd.

Rnd 3: *P1 A, drop A, bring B *under* A and p1 B, drop B, bring A *under* B; rep from * to marker.

Outer band:

Rnd 1: With C, knit.
Rnd 2: With A, knit.
Rnd 3: With B, knit.
Rep these 3 rnds 2 more times.
Next Rnd: With C, knit.

Work second braid as first.

Hatband: Using markers, divide 114 sts into 6 groups of 19 sts each. Work each group with a different background color. Knit 4 rnds of each background color, then inc 1 st before and after each marker. Follow Chart 1 using A for contrast color—198 sts. Cut all background colors and join B. Work third braid as before.

Points: *Underside:* Divide sts into 3 sections of 66 sts each. Place 2 sections on holders and work 1 section at a time. Knit one row, inc 1 st—67 sts. Knit the underside of each point in St st, dec 1 st at each end of every other row, until 3 sts rem. Place 3 sts on holder.

Top side: Place 3 sts from holder on needle. Knit back down the points, increasing each side every other row by picking up a st from the underside where you decreased on the way up. When you have 67 sts, place on holder. Work rem 2 points. Knit the 3 points into a rnd, knitting the last st from 1 point tog with the first st of next point—198 sts.

Work another braid as before.

With CC knit 3 rnds.

Next rnd: [k4, k2tog, k3, k2tog] 18 times—162 sts.

Knit 1 rnd.

Crown: Follow Chart 2.

Finishing: With color A, knit 4 bobbles as follows:

CO 8 sts on dpns. Join, being careful not to twist sts.

Rnd 1: Knit.

Rnd 2: *M1, k2; rep from *—12 sts.

Rnd 3: Knit.

Rnd 4: *M1, k1; rep from *—24 sts.

Rnds 5 and 6: Knit.

Rnd 7: *K2tog; rep from *—12 sts.

Stuff the little pouch you're knitting with bits of fleece.

Rnd 8: *K2tog; rep from *—6 sts.

Cut yarn, leaving a tail and sew up rem sts. Sew one bobble to the end of each point and one at top.

Chart 1

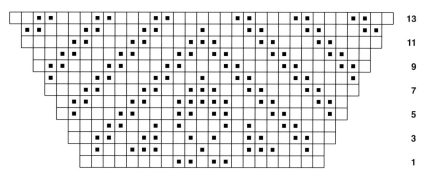

Chart 2

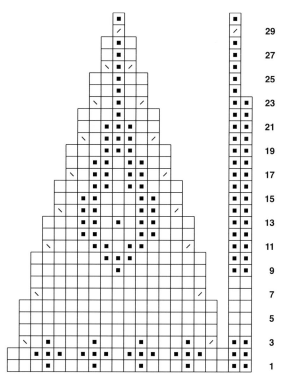

	color A
＼	ssk on RS; ssp on WS
／	k2tog on RS; p2 tog on WS

Tops With a Twist

Dreaming of the Garden

Catherine Reimes
Lancaster, New York

Embroidery turns bobbles into "beebles" on this fun child's hat.

YARN: Ready-spun colored roving in various small amounts (light green, dark green, pink, brown, lavender, yellow, plum, cream, dark brown, orange).

NEEDLES: Size 2 (2.75 mm) 16" circular (cir) and 3 (3.25 mm) 16" cir and double-pointed (dpn).

GAUGE: 10 sts = 2" (5 cm).

NOTIONS: Size F crochet; tapestry needle.

Stitches

Mini-bobble stitch:
[P1, k1, p1, k1] into next st, pass 2nd, 3rd and 4th sts over 1st st.

Beebles:
Using crochet hook, go down into fabric at one end of "wings" (cream background already knitted). Pull up loop of yarn and anchor to hat. Pull up about 8 loops. Hold base of loops, turn hook down and pull yarn through all the loops (this is also called a crocheted "popcorn"). To fasten, pull yarn end through, turn and position beeble, and knot.

With light green and smaller needle, CO 72 sts.

Rnds 1 through 8: Work corrugated rib (k1 light green, p1 dark green). Change to larger needle and follow chart to end changing colors and slipping sts as indicated.

Earflaps: With dark green, pick up 16 sts on either side of hat. Work 4 rows St st, then dec as follows:

Row 1: (RS) Ssk, k to last 2 sts, k2tog.

Row 2: Purl.

Rep last 2 rows until 8 sts rem. BO all sts. With crochet hook, ch35, sc up earflap and around front of hat to bottom of other earflap, chain 35, SC around rest of hat.

Embroidery

Bees: With dark brown, embroider one straight stitch for head and two across body for stripes on beebles.

Carrots and lettuce: Alternate the two evenly spaced around the hat in the brown space.

Carrots: For orange part, make one long daisy stitch, fill in the center with one straight stitch if necessary. With light green, embroider carrot tops in straight stitch.

Lettuce: Anchor as for beebles, ch2, anchor in fabric, ch2, tie both ends tog and finish off.

Top "button": Using lavender, work as for lettuce but ch3 instead of ch2.

The Trickster's Hat

Jacqueline D. Vaughan
and
Nika Vaughan
Lansing, Michigan

A mother and daughter team created this hat. Nika attends the Art Institue of Chicago; she designed the figure and I figured out how to use him in the hat. When I first saw the figure, I thought of a Shaman's hat. I then thought of the "Anasi the Spider" stories from West African folklore that I had read to my children. I took Nika's "trickster" and super-imposed him on graph paper, then designed the hat around him. I used natural clay beads for his eyes so that "Mr. Bonee" could come alive. The hat is oversized for those of us with very thick, curly hair.

YARN: 6 oz. silk/camel blend (beige), 6 oz. alpaca/silk blend (black).

NEEDLES: Size 1 (2.25 mm) and 2 (2.75 mm) 16" circular.

GAUGE: 14 sts and 16 rows = 2" (5 cm).

NOTIONS: Four natural clay beads for eyes; tapestry needle.

Stitches

Bobble: Knit into back, front, back, front, and back of stitch, turn; sl 1, p4, turn; sl 1, k4, turn; pass 4 sts over last st; turn and continue rnd.

With black and smaller needle, CO 144 sts. Join beige and follow chart through row 12. Change to larger needle and continue to follow chart.

Top of hat:

Rnd 1: With black, *sl 1, k1, psso, k18, k2tog, k2; rep from *—132 sts.

Rnds 2 and 14: *K5, make bobble; rep from *.

Rnds 3 and 15: Knit.

Rnd 4: With beige, *k2tog, k9; rep from *—120 sts.

Rnd 5: *K1 beige, k1 black; rep from *.

Rnds 6 and 17: *K1 black, k1 beige; rep from *.

Rnd 7: With black, *k2tog, k4; rep from *—100 sts.

Rnds 8 and 9: With black, knit.

Rnd 10: With beige, *k2tog, k3; rep from *—80 sts.

Rnd 11: *K2 black, k2 beige; rep from *.

Rnds 12, 16, and 18: With beige, knit.

Rnds 13, 19, 21, and 25: With black, knit.

Rnd 14: With black, *k4, make bobble; rep from *.

Rnd 15: With black, *k2tog, k2; rep from *—60 sts.

Rnd 20: With black, *k2 tog, k3; rep from *—48 sts.

Rnds 22, 24, and 26: With beige, knit.

Rnd 23: With black, *k2tog, k2; rep from *—36 sts.

Rnd 27: With black, *k2tog, k1; rep from *—24 sts.

Break yarn leaving an 8" (20.5-cm) tail. Thread tail on tapestry needle and run through rem sts. Secure. Weave in loose ends.

Tops With a Twist

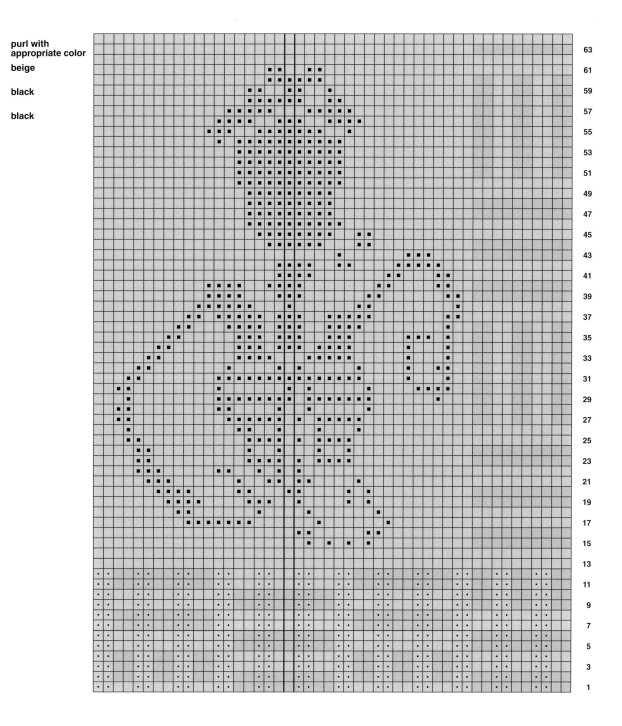

Index

abbreviations 11

Bakriges, Jean 17

Ballerino, Diane 21

Bertino, Karen 25

bullion circle 25 – 26

charts, reading 11

Christophel, Crik 28

Copeland, Lauri 31

Cosell, Lynn 34

Crawford, Susan 37

crochet chain cast-on 12 – 13

crochet chain stitch 11

daisy stitch 13

Doe, Carolyn 40

double crochet 11 – 12

Douglas, Susan Z. 44

embroidery 13

Friedrichsen, Verna 47, 50

Gwinner, Lisa 53

I-cord 13

Inda, Jean 57

Kitchener stitch 14

M1 increase 14

Miller, Sarah 59

Miriam, Selma 63

Murray, Hazel 67

O'Donnell, Leah 59

Reimes, Catherine 73

single crochet 12

slip stitch crochet 12

straight stitch 13

tassels 28

Vaughan, Jacqueline D. 75

Vaughan, Nika 75

wrapping a stitch 14 – 15

yarn butterfly 15

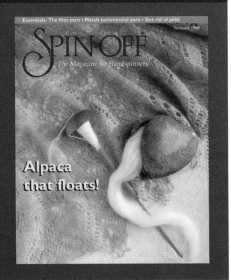